INTO THE WORDS
AS WORDS ARE FOR FOREVER

SHARDHA JAIN

Copyright © Shardha Jain
All Rights Reserved.

ISBN 978-1-68586-383-8

This book has been published with all efforts taken to make the material error-free after the consent of the author. However, the author and the publisher do not assume and hereby disclaim any liability to any party for any loss, damage, or disruption caused by errors or omissions, whether such errors or omissions result from negligence, accident, or any other cause.

While every effort has been made to avoid any mistake or omission, this publication is being sold on the condition and understanding that neither the author nor the publishers or printers would be liable in any manner to any person by reason of any mistake or omission in this publication or for any action taken or omitted to be taken or advice rendered or accepted on the basis of this work. For any defect in printing or binding the publishers will be liable only to replace the defective copy by another copy of this work then available.

I dedicate this book to the readers, who may after reading my thoughts & experiences may derive some meaningful aspects towards their life.

This book is also dedicated to my family & few friends for believing in me and encouraging me to present my thoughts.

Contents

Preface   *vii*

About The Author   *ix*

SEARCHING SELF

   1. Collect Your Pieces   3

   2. Observe To Understand   19

   3. Silence Speaks   29

   4. Thoughts Matters   42

   5. Holding Skies   51

THE ONLY JOURNEY

   6. Life Is Forever Journey   63

   7. Time Is Wonderful   75

   8. Books Are Roads To Mind   87

   9. Writing Life With Words   100

   10. Everything Is Written   109

STUPID EMOTIONS

   11. Feelings Are Like Clouds   119

   12. Control Your Emotions   127

   13. Healing   137

   14. Language Of Soul   145

   15. Wishes   155

LIGHT WITHIN

   16. Keep Shining   165

   17. Light Isn't Illusion   174

   18. Reality Is Candle   183

Contents

19. Beauty Of Life	191
20. Be The Spark	201
The Author's Mission	213

Preface

This is my very first book expressing my perceptions and experiences about life & it's ways. Being a soul with a curious mind has always me made to find meanings out of words. I don't believe easily on any thing as having strong faith in my conscience but this sometimes also got me into trouble. I never learnt to give up. I always believe that what's happening is in surely in our hands always but we failed to observe and start judging the situations rather than outcomes. Words can colour the canvas without colours & explain emotions without senses. Just a single word can tell the whole story. There's nothing magical & powerful than meaningful words. But most of the people often neglects the beauty of words that attracts soul and make us humane & kind. This book may help readers to find hidden meanings of words that are so meaningful & magical to change our vision.

> *"Be a person of words,*
> *As words are for forever."*

About The Author

A Nature lover, Bibliophile that has lot to say but this practical world just don't get her. A Chemistry teacher by profession but writer by chance, maybe being introvert.

A Native of holy city, Rishikesh and strong believer of truth and honesty. A simple soul who just never give up. Paper has more patience than people all she believes. She is Shardha Jain (Pen Name - Shrain), who prefers to dive into words rather than ersatz worldliness. She has written in many anthologies - "Tremendous Words", "Ignited Soul", "World Of Words", "Mind Maze" and many more are under process of publication. She is compiler of "The Words Of Instinct" and "Stupid Emotions".

ABOUT THE AUTHOR

"Handle them carefully,

for words have more power

than atom bombs."

-Pearl Strachan Hurd

"Words have energy and power

with the ability to help, to heal,

to hinder, to hurt, to harm,

to humiliate, and to humble."

-Yehuda Berg

SEARCHING SELF

1
Collect Your Pieces

Be self,
try to be original and real,
that's the key to peace.

INTO THE WORDS

*What we carry inside
is more important for self than others,
Because whether it's light or heavy,
only we have to carry.*

Learn to stop during the journey,
to measure the courage & patience.

INTO THE WORDS

Try to be fine with stitched broken glasses,
Hold the heart without bandages.

*Heartily ways are not so easy
to be supported & pursued
in ersatz thinking world.*

Our happiness is not necessarily other's liking also.

*Just believe in yourself
as no one is companion
to your journey,
it's you & your's only.*

INTO THE WORDS

When life seems to beat you down,
Hold the breath to dodge it.

Some people change when options ends and life starts.

INTO THE WORDS

*From above,
it looks scary
from where it all started.*

SHARDHA JAIN

*Let them leave
and
make your flight more light.*

*My eyes see differently
now today,
When I opened eyes
rather than heart.*

*When life goes backwards hold the surrounding tightly
and
improve the canvas.*

Some doors are better closed than open ones to avoid fall in traps.

*It's good to observe
than to react,
To avoid misjudge & misinterprets.*

INTO THE WORDS

Let us find
Self rather than others.
Furnish with failures
than regrets.

2
Observe To Understand

*Life is'nt a straight road
it's a bend
whenever mistakenly assumed
straight.*

INTO THE WORDS

*Fear is a strange thing
as it makes strong
and
tough than ever.*

Everything is planned
and
everything is written,
We are just never ready for it.

INTO THE WORDS

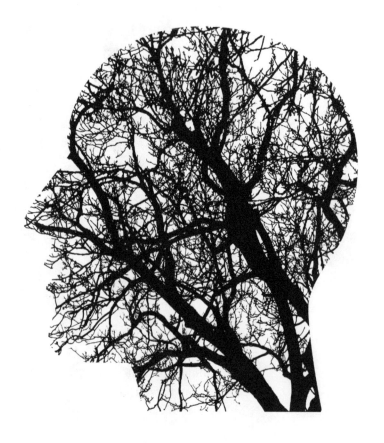

The worldliness is so captive for our free souls.

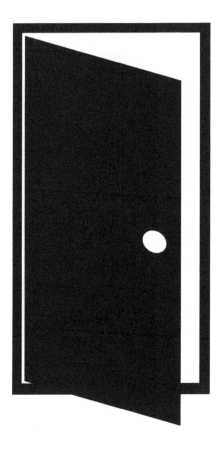

Quitting a habit is like ignoring the open door.

INTO THE WORDS

*Life is a jar
where to think of
escape
will give punishment
by destiny.*

In hope for a change of situations,
We've changed ourself.

INTO THE WORDS

*Heart holds a secret corner
where we used to pile up all desires and sentiments.*

*Life is a staircase
that is ready to tire us
on every step,
So that we can understand
it's actual importance.*

INTO THE WORDS

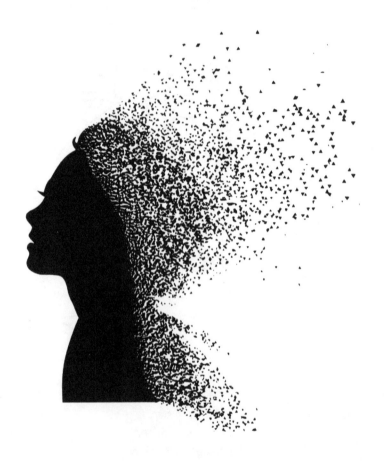

Vision is important than eyes,
Like thoughts are important than mind.

3
Silence Speaks

*If night were a person
then silence is it's soulmate.*

29

INTO THE WORDS

*Be like fireflies
make presence by your light,
no matter of the depth of dark
or the extent of your light.*

On that lone street
loneliness proves the best companion ever,
listening to our thoughts without doubts.

INTO THE WORDS

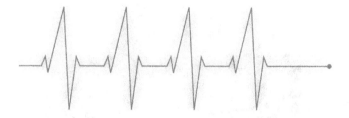

*I hear the whispers
of silence
talking of Rhythm
and beats of Heart.*

*Heartily ways are not so easy
to be supported & pursued
in ersatz thinking world.*

INTO THE WORDS

*When there is darkness
there is enlightenment of
instinct & soul
as it's the only option remained.*

*Moon explains the meanings
of silence to dark.*

INTO THE WORDS

Some nights come in hopes that some words in shadow can really be spoken.

SHARDHA JAIN

*Loneliness is temporary boring,
But it's trustworthy friend.*

INTO THE WORDS

Night cries in sorrow
of loneliness
each & every time
on the shoulders of silence.

SHARDHA JAIN

When there is no way,
there is blind faith
in the roads crowded by silence.

INTO THE WORDS

*When darkness knocks,
it want to tell you stories
full of silence.*

The night listens to those
those that knows
the lyrics of silence.

4
Thoughts Matters

*Our thoughts don't need
an agreement from anyone.*

The sunlight crawls into my room like
giving indication to my thoughts
to a path.

*It's better unsaid than thousands
heavy misinterprets
and
blames.*

*Darkness contains the vibes
that don't needs any shine
but only a conscience.*

INTO THE WORDS

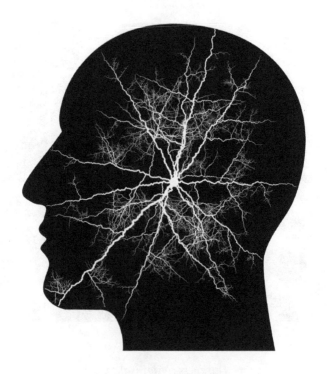

*Between the mind & heart,
everything is in imbalance
and chaotic,
With the mind & heart,
everything is in balance & peaceful.*

Nobody understands us better than the written words.

INTO THE WORDS

*Thoughts
can't be controlled
but
their direction
can be.*

*When it rain, I feel
that it's better to shed
than to hold for too long,
to analyse the heaviness.*

INTO THE WORDS

*We became cold,
when perceptions turned misinterprets.*

5
Holding Skies

Raindrops carry the weights of emotions of clouds.

INTO THE WORDS

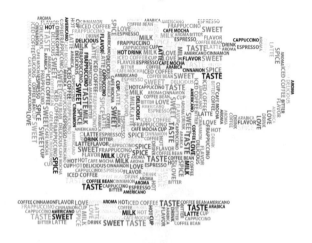

*Busy in world of words
where everything
keeps a meaning.*

Some things are always changed,
Whenever we look back.

INTO THE WORDS

*A little ray of sunshine is enough
to prove the existence to the dark.*

*You can't apply
everything going on in head.*

INTO THE WORDS

Beauty lies in thoughts
and
the way we treat other beings.

Little little eyes
Holding all the skies.

INTO THE WORDS

A click holds the humanity of moment.

Meanings are always too hard,
Misinterprets are just too easy.

INTO THE WORDS

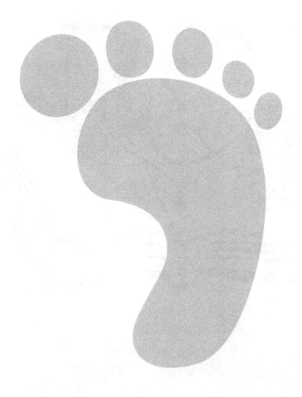

*Gone time always becomes
shadows & impressions
to remind it.*

THE ONLY JOURNEY

6
Life is Forever Journey

*A life without attachments is better
than depression & regrets.*

INTO THE WORDS

*In life, some lessons are
uninvited and
just deep
to cut deep
the soul
with
non-healing scars.*

*When life gives you wings,
practice properly
before high jump.*

INTO THE WORDS

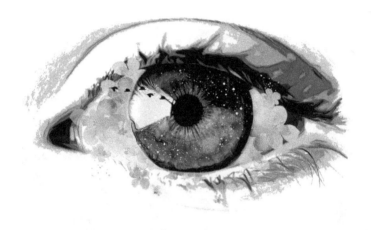

Life begins with everything
and
losing one by one
everything.

Life is that deadly game
that always gives
toughest competition
to make you fail everytime.

INTO THE WORDS

*We all keep chasing the fantasies of
our thoughts,
But finally we have to accept
the reality droughts.*

*We understand life
when we fail to understand
our own words.*

INTO THE WORDS

Too Long times of patience,
No interest in ambience.

When the world seems rude,
Just demand the love from God.

INTO THE WORDS

*We all are passengers
with no actual destination.*

*Life becomes simple when
nothing really matters,
meaning of efforts become clear.*

INTO THE WORDS

*Just roads beyond roads,
Life is forever journey.*

7
Time is Wonderful

—♡—

*Time is like flooded water,
just only in hurry
without caring anything in it's way.*

INTO THE WORDS

*Time favours those
who are in hunger of future.*

*Gone time always becomes
shadows & impressions
to remind it.*

*Night seems short
when there is lot to discuss with silence.*

*Be the first to climb fears
before anyone else.*

Something always left,
That's the problem
of memories.

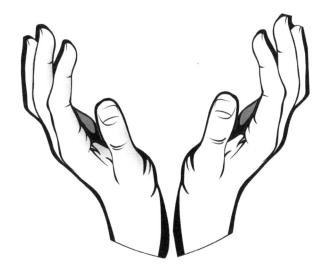

*Time is too slippery
to stand & observe.*

INTO THE WORDS

*Past is that chapter
which always demands some forgets.*

SHARDHA JAIN

*More the old are the things,
more research is needed.*

*Memories are always killing,
as we can't touch them again.*

*Time is too slow
to forget regrets.*

INTO THE WORDS

*Time is the currency
often used with stinginess.*

8
Books Are Roads To Mind

*Books are the keys
to the words
missed in our
vocabulary.*

*You need to burn
those whole chapters
that proves you.
guilty constantly.*

*Turning page is'nt so facile,
Not everytime happens with smile.*

INTO THE WORDS

*Some times we don't have
any single word
in skull to explain.*

*Books are a gateway to some real
and
meaningful words.*

INTO THE WORDS

*Fantasies are just only
beautiful illusions.*

*Some people come with
lots of lessons,
that one can compile them
enough as a book.*

INTO THE WORDS

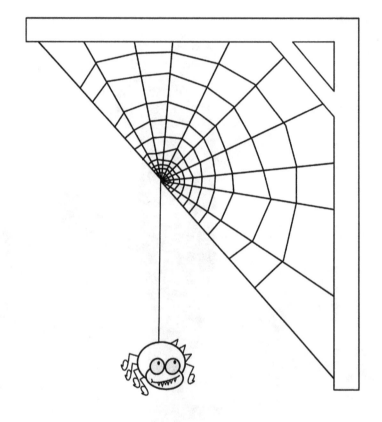

*Books help you to get some
real corners.*

*Books are not just to read
the lines or words,
it's for the diving into
the depth of ocean of meanings.*

INTO THE WORDS

*Books are friends
with zero benefits
and zero betrayal
and infinite confidence.*

Books are the infinite clouds
where we can fly
with wings of thoughts & words.

INTO THE WORDS

*Books are not enough
for those unable to find
meanings in words.*

*Between the lines of book,
something is always present
to hit instinct directly.*

9
Writing Life with Words

*We generally writes those things
that are hard to forget.*

*Writing fills
the voids of heart.*

INTO THE WORDS

The silence of night contains
the words in shadow.

On the blank pages,
there is lots of patience
to hold the heaviness of words.

INTO THE WORDS

*Writing makes
shadowed words of instinct
to come in light.*

A corner where we express
everything true.
Just one moment of bliss
is like a stone
thrown in silent water.

We stay in the dark corners of our shadows of thoughts.

*A writer is simply a mind,
penning thoughts as words
to be understand by readers.*

INTO THE WORDS

*It's important to
write reality that
nobody wants to accept
But curious to read.*

10
Everything Is Written

*Everything is planned
and
everything is written,*

INTO THE WORDS

We are just never ready for it.

*Learn from past
that original never
costs & meant too much.*

*Nobody understands us better
than than the written words.*

INTO THE WORDS

*Reading introduces to
the concealed
world of words.*

*Reading helps in reducing
overthinking
by giving our thoughts
a point of disembarkation.*

INTO THE WORDS

Everyone has stories to tell
but
there is no listener around.

*Even darkness is important
to feel the missing words
in the ocean of life.*

INTO THE WORDS

*Endings are beautiful
when it marks the feeling of healing
and
letting go.*

STUPID EMOTIONS

11
Feelings Are Like Clouds

*No one can control,
what we really desires.*

Between present and past,
We have killed our
stupid real emotions.

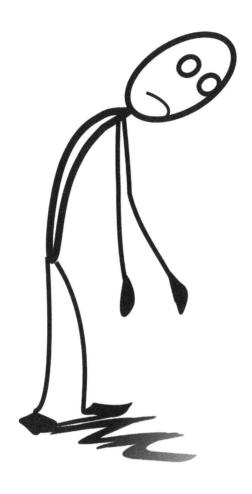

*Regrets are the painful
hidden emotions
that are always
empty of words.*

Heart's a vacant place
to all wasted emotions.

SHARDHA JAIN

*My heart wants to follow
the route of
happiness & joy,
But mind always
shuts up.*

Game of Emotions is more lethal than any other game.

SHARDHA JAIN

*Being special
is biggest illusion.*

INTO THE WORDS

*What makes me confident is my god presence
in every harsh hour.*

12
Control Your Emotions

All is a Stupid?
If it's for the Heart ♥?
Thoughts are mind rapid??
Making the intelligence outsmart?

We all grow from real smiles to fake ones.

*Rain brings back
millions of thoughts,
emotions & memories
in it's pure drops.*

*Be the vibe that controls heart
but not emotions.*

*World has no place for emotions
and
rhythms of heart.*

INTO THE WORDS

*When it comes to heart,
I'm learning to quiet
it's rhythms,
emotions & rush of
excitements.*

*A poet is someone who try to stitch fragile emotions
and voiceless words
in the ocean of
patience of paper.*

INTO THE WORDS

*Lost things & lost emotions
are never found again.*

*Don't forget to water the emotions,
that are heart speaks.*

INTO THE WORDS

*The essence of life is
is being in real in reality
beyond ersatz smiles & emotions,
that are just wasted.*

13
Healing

*Imaginations have infinite range,
can make or break the emotions.*

Healing comes from moving on,
rather than standing
and
blocking the path.

Some things demands talks,
Inspite of avoids.

INTO THE WORDS

*We all are hidden world,
But only some dares to explore.*

Don't speak too much,
It's philosophy according to today.

INTO THE WORDS

*A new day bring Is
an opportunity to
improve mistakes.*

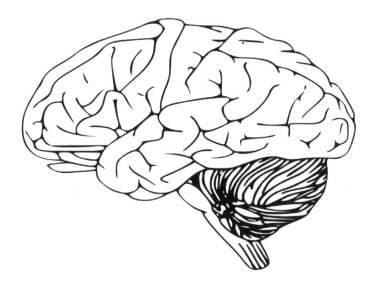

*Not all colours are needed
to paint the canvas of mind.*

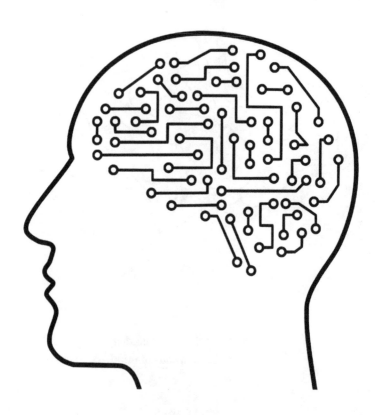

*Never merge your thoughts with others,
It will modify originality & values.*

14
Language Of Soul

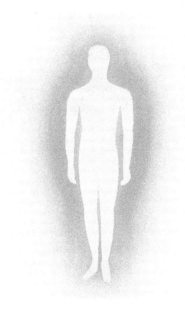

All what my soul craves for true kind behaves,
For the whole Ocean,
Not only just waves.

INTO THE WORDS

*Only the heart knows
the fading rhythms,
hides & shadowed words
that are actually
relatable to soul.*

*Sometimes, only silence can explain
the screaming soul.*

Standing at the edge of truth & reality,
Only offering my soul fatality.

*Soul can't befriend
mind and heart at the same time.*

INTO THE WORDS

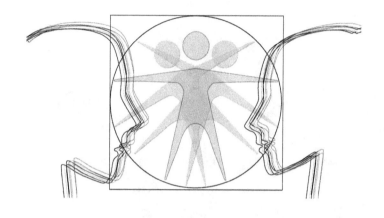

*Every living contains same soul,
but with different ways.*

*Meanings always produce
vibrations in soul.*

INTO THE WORDS

*Not every soul blossoms
to become flower.*

*Don't allow thoughts to make soul suffer,
control them with positive attitude.*

INTO THE WORDS

*Words can affect
the soul profoundly.*

15
Wishes

Each tiny wish carries lots of emotions.

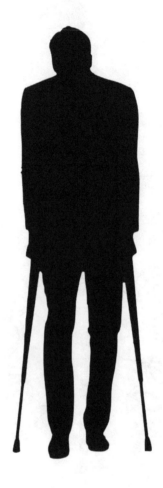

*Don't look broken,
people generally make wish
out of broken things.*

*Expectations die when
we actually learn
to accept
reality of world.*

INTO THE WORDS

A little hope is O. K.
But a lot of hope
is always killing.

SHARDHA JAIN

*Self care is a medicine to cure disease
"Expectations".*

*Clouds often take shape of imaginations,
without fear.*

*There are no
castles of happiness.*

INTO THE WORDS

*Like cat's eyes
all impressions are
just camouflage.*

LIGHT WITHIN

16
Keep Shining

*Don't become a bouquet
for someone appreciation.*

INTO THE WORDS

The ending must be an end,
Not a repeating story.

*In the world of infinite stars,
don't wish for just a moon.*

When we understand self value,
No one can stop us ever.

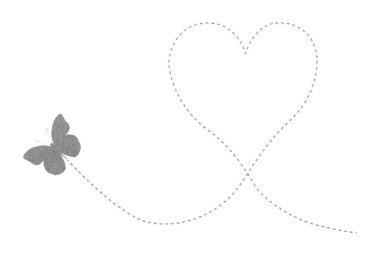

Happiness comes to those who forget about details & interest of it.

INTO THE WORDS

*The true wisdom is
to know what real things mean
rather than being.*

*Be the flowing water
not stagnant one.*

INTO THE WORDS

*We aren't just a body
but a soul to be responsible.*

*Don't get emotional ever,
Just keep it in.*

17
Light Isn't Illusion

*Fill your life with
your self,
Not with the other's fake
matter of illusions.*

SHARDHA JAIN

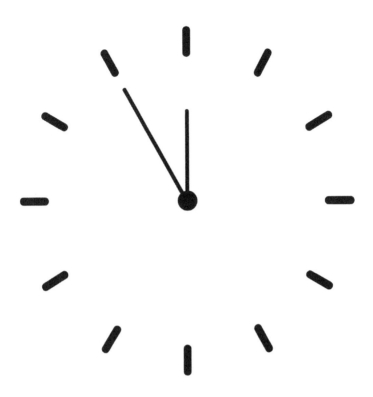

*Sometimes keeping a secret
is too burdened,
That makes killing
at every ticks of clock.*

INTO THE WORDS

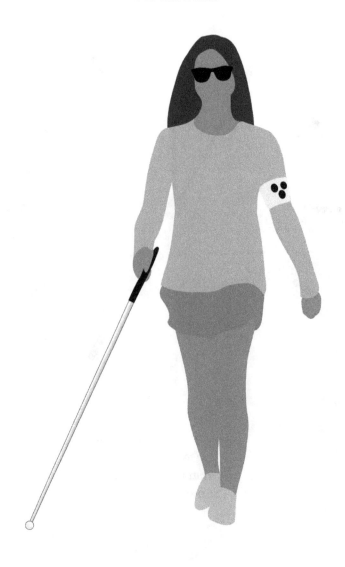

*Blind paths are the paths not taken
by common.*

*When you keep trying,
you will get millions
of phases
to test patience.*

INTO THE WORDS

The sky tries to tell the
the story of blind
believes & believers.

*Sunsets are
reminders
that ends are must
to ponder & start again.*

*Don't think what other's will think,
Think what can be done to improve.*

Let your light shine
Not for others only,
But for you firstly.

INTO THE WORDS

There's nothing wrong in light light.
Till when it don't make blind.

18
Reality Is Candle

*In search of
Humanity,
I lost my own.*

INTO THE WORDS

Don't expect from everyone,
Not everyone is a good reader.

*There is no home
on the roads of life.*

INTO THE WORDS

*Don't bother for a hand
to lend & depend,
as it often push into the abyss.*

*One thing I love about travelling is that it's exactly similar to life,
it explains that to reach somewhere,
we have to leave from here.*

INTO THE WORDS

Not all views are gratifying,
Some are just optional.

Trust is that delicate flower which withers with winds of betrayal.

*Courage is Only option,
when everything is just inimical.*

19
Beauty Of Life

*Life is beautiful like roses,
including thorns.*

INTO THE WORDS

*In the world of infinite stars,
don't wish for just a moon.*

Beauty doesn't define reality,
It hides only originality.

*The Beauty of simplicity is immense & weightless,
It's only felt, not explained.*

Sometimes we opt wrongest path by following attractions.

INTO THE WORDS

*Not every sparkles meant
to be a star.*

*Beauty is not always
true and kind.*

Not all smiles are just smiles.

Nature contains beauty
in sunshine
as well as darkness.

INTO THE WORDS

Forever is a magician
who just vanishes
after the words.

20
Be The Spark

A Spark is enough to ignite the soul.

INTO THE WORDS

Emotions spark the essence of our character.

Words sparks meanings in mind,
To clear the fogs of skepticism.

INTO THE WORDS

*Don't hide the flames
of your natural skills.*

*Let's find things
that ignite the mind
and the soul.*

*Positive thinking ignites
the state of mind
towards meanings.*

*Books cast spark
to infinite imaginations.*

INTO THE WORDS

*Mental pictures ignites thoughts
that are only controlled by attitude.*

We can be the whole sun,
If the spark obstinate to burn.

INTO THE WORDS

Burn like fire
but express like ice.

*Lights are reason for
sensation of vision,
But not for doors to wisdom.*

The Author's Mission

I hope that readers find something purposeful after reading this book during their journey into the world of words. Words are everything if we intents to be true beyond any situations. I will feel gratitude if some find meanings after reading my thoughts and experiences. We all deserve to find meanings of life that resonates our soul.

You can post pages, quotes,thoughts and experiences related to my book "INTO THE WORDS", so that I can feature them on my social page on instagram @shrainquotes (My pen name is Shrain).

CPSIA information can be obtained
at www.ICGtesting.com
Printed in the USA
LVHW031937250122
709218LV00007B/515